WHETHERING

The Colorado Prize for Poetry

RUSTY MORRISON

WHETHERING

POEMS

Center
for
Literary
Publishing
Fort Collins

For information about permission
to reproduce selections from this book,
write to Permissions, Center for Literary Publishing,
Department of English, Colorado State University,
Fort Collins, Colorado 80523.

Set in Copperplate and Bulmer.
Printed in the United States of America.
Cover designed by Quemadura.

Library of Congress Cataloging-in-Publication Data

Morrison, Rusty.
   Whethering : poems / Rusty Morrison.
      p. cm. -- (The Colorado prize)
   Includes bibliographical references.
   ISBN 1-885635-07-9 (pbk. : alk. paper)
   I. Title. II. Series.

   PS3613.O7777W48 2004
   811'.6--dc22

                              2004018534

The paper used in this book meets the minimum
requirements of the American National Standard
for Information Sciences-Permanence of Paper
for Printed Library Materials, ANSI Z39.48-1984.

1 2 3 4 5   08 07 06 05 04

To Ken

We must watch passing clouds. Time's fixed on nothingness.

—Vera Linhartová

CONTENTS

ACKNOWLEDGMENTS

Some poems have changed in title or form and first appeared in *Web Conjunctions* ("Escape Sequence," "Morning Sequence," and "Caution Sequence"), *New American Writing* ("Field Notes: 13–20"), *Poetry Flash* ("Mistake Sequence"), *SLOPE* ("The *sporadic-proverbial* Grasp series"), and *Ur Vox* ("Field Notes: 1–6").

Two of these poem sequences were finalists in the 2003 *New Letters* Literary Awards: the "Making Space" and "Climate Conditional" sequences.

Many thanks to the Djerassi Artists Residency Program, where these poem cycles began.

My heartfelt thanks to the fine writers who have given the poems in this manuscript their wise and perceptive attention: Robin Caton, Patricia Dienstfrey, Grace Grafton, Brenda Hillman, Melissa Kwasny, and Elizabeth Robinson. Much gratitude to Forrest Gander for selecting these poems.

WHETHERING

CLIMATE CONDITIONAL (MORNING FORECAST)

whethering which is to say waking is only one thing
stumbles too late behind the other making

dimensions real
this portioned space

white soap in its dish bathroom window open to
autumn frost intellect silent with

before
enormous crow rides in on the nerves of a motionless

actual
streetlamp ticks dark what I construct

distance to feel
arrival

fused to next I lean like horizon
the end pull

fills in the tedium with follow
measures ecstasy with cotton cloth steamy

water in the tub
Expansive

but what can sustain

ESCAPE SEQUENCE

Bees in the notebook,
which were easier than birds to draw,

a sexual reference to what won't be heard.   Idea intersects
and idea insects
both hum

when I'd wanted simple weight and sweat,
to taste and be done with it.

Lips invade evasively, never just two,   collision is
sometimes subtle as breath
against breath, and how far to press the inner,

softer flesh   is not choice but collusion.

After. Which I have too much of
to make the word mean it.
On our backs
in the sun. Grass stings with every blade not the same
and all at once,   what it gives.

Reedy grass in this yard.   And weeds
in chaotic growth spirals.
Here, the dirt is also hard and we go to it for the capture
of what skin can feel.

No one, which is everything listening.

You is a word for it.

This harder than sky. This world, meaning always
some other one,
before it reverts back, or worse, strays. Not the parallel,
but the scatter.

Though we lie through our smiles. Sweet

absenting. We call it
talk.

Now it's quiet, just the wind,

like a wanting we fall through,   close your eyes.

Your back and shoulders
I fit my breasts to,
and then where to put this knee, wrist, a woodenness
unfolds the tongue inside the mouth,

finds and finds.   What it won't touch, talisman
of impossible shelter,

empty point I rely on   outside perception.

FIELD NOTES: 1–6

*[A] sum but not a whole, Nature is not attributive, but rather
conjunctive: it expresses itself through "and" . . .*
—Gilles Deleuze

*And around the thing the word hovers freely, like a soul
around a body that has been abandoned but not forgotten.*
—Osip Mandelstam

—cloudless sky   what will not yield to memory

expands   opposite of seeing   all tang   no tangled
                              into discernible
the after-image of being
isn't reason

—spider's web in wind   stretched the width of a trail

here is resemblance
that erasure

                              if kept curious   will linger
at the threshold before pattern   becomes experience

—feint tearing in two   sound of

rabbit from no rabbit   asks   not even wind
gone in thick
    as trail-dusted underbrush   as whither the meaning
from the thing said

—that motive   which stillness in the landscape acquires

depiction   spiders its skein
            of thought across the seen
a perspective
eliminates   not illuminates   the looking

—horizon illusion

made with god poultices   whatever will draw
   ransom a little dove under cloud
                        say significance   think
it sight   when vision would be opaque and endless

—redwood's fissured bark   the artery

of a lark's cry   no clear path through the tactic of no other
than this
          and make it mean   sweat brings me
back to skin
       to outline's porosity

MAKING SPACE

. . . life is the unknown essence concealed in the space
which supports it.
—I. Rice Pereira

I. A HORTICULTURE

teeth we grow daily   one at a time   virtue names
each of them   hands come up in the night
     like weeds   their seed heads and flower spikes
name themselves   we don't expect listening   some nights
so loud   din of the personal impersonating us
     our yard is wild grass and poppies   but we are thick
with the foliage of the body's fright

                    ROOTS ENDLESSLY ORIENTING

          TURN ALONG THE ANGLE OF SPACE

in evening light   tree branches ink outside the lines
     you study our trellis vines   their knack for redistributing
essence   I listen for what describing interrupts   a purple-ish
bud of fixity in each shifting reference   we share a hard
yellow cheese a glass of wine   but skin is a risk in dusk's easy
ungainliness   jittery leaf dark scratches your lips against mine
     we briar and bruise   how to stay nimble and changeless
as salt   as appearance

                    LEFT SENTIENT   UNOCCUPIED

II. HOUSE HOLDING SPACE

tonight we're busy domesticating magnitudes   I pencil-sharpen
a greeting   you grocery-list as a kind of finesse   how differently
we pronounce mopped floor dusted table tops vacuumed corners
clean is so hard to listen for   ruined by polish   no simple
sameness in predicting rainfall or migration's pull or familial
fastidiousness   our pile of forgotten wet laundry might dry
into a map of a labyrinth   or a war

BY DISORIENTATION   THAT INCOGNITO FIXATIVE

ONLY VARIOUSNESS

hands follow patterns made visible only at a distance with
the superior hilarity of dream   I didn't say body parts
but ramparts   which comes from the Old Provençal "amparar"
meaning "to prepare"   close one eye for accuracy
and lose dimension   even safe in our room
there will always be trees we have no names for
growing out of our closet

IMPELS SENSATION

III. IF WE

sitting in our car at the Berkeley Marina   drinking wine
from paper cups   late afternoon extending its parameters
tempting us to fill them   we knew better   that's what
you said   but even the saying   takes up the place of three gulls
riding an updraft   but not the fourth   whose long arching wings
have already slipped behind whatever slid back together
and steadied away from us   into nothing we could call a direction

SUSTAIN A FALLING LIKE WATER'S

INTO THE SOURCE OF SPACE

never ignore slippage   isn't that what you said
    whether it comes in the shapes we believe in or the ones
we don't   but we were awkward under the shadow that wine
had lent us   a little out of focus in the snapshots of ego
that are conversation   which we nonetheless
collect   our brief sequence of startle   disguised as stillness
    measuring our need for clarity against the pleasing pulse
of its interruption

FLOW IS ALTERNATIVE TO DIRECTION

IV. DUSK

walking the fire trail along Strawberry Creek   walking as a frame
we use to pull the moon through our memories
of its photograph   here are berries   black as the finitude images
take and take   will not give back   we measure
each wanting against the shape of the last   dried mud crumbles
under our shoes   fragile red rivulets

VIBRANT OPENINGS OF SPACE

WHERE MIND RESISTS

what threatens us   perilous wilderness of permissions
    I say free-flight but I see only birds moving deeper
inside the empty depths of bird   after twilight
we visit the lake   geese everywhere asleep in the grass
    and sky all in the language of sky   unwilling
to engage in translation

WE CATCH ONLY MOVEMENT

V. THE OLDEST DEVICE

I can explain to you about the gradual dissolve   lips meet
at the small "o"   volatile   not
devotional   still the inadvertent blush
is kin to grandeur   we alternate
by walking on tiptoes   not the small wound   just saying so

SHADOW AND LIGHT

IN DIRECT OBSERVATION

but you have put the problem another way
     swaying grass appeases nothing
but the surety of its own expression
     now   not a meaning for now   later
we'll paint the kitchen   line the cabinets
     buy a new teakettle   but the first madness
is the same   I always find it
     imagine I might make of it the rest of my life

WHAT DIMINISHES IS SPACE

CLIMATE CONDITIONAL (EVENING FORECAST)

a mind makes dusk
a raccoon

quick in the near brush
    his eye heavily populated

    nonlinear his horizon line
I see only one red sun

call it time
    invert body to invent a word

    reach out a hand
and already day isn't

its tone remains evenly pitched
    like a summons the same

    foreignness in conviction
as in cravings

which abjure translating guideposts
    What I refuse I construe

    as absence
fills every space

I empty to explain it

RISK SEQUENCE

Here's a word sealed in its sentence,   a perfect row

of one-shot tequila bottles
               behind the counter top's glass,
beside the convenience store's cash register,

tells nothing   except the past

is never the way I want to remember it.
And the present
passes into haze   beside more articulated

points of reference. These   boasting easy-open screw tops

and "especial" right on the label.

Passes like sky
changes into weather.   The kind that rains

inside each bottle,
won't pour out.
A heavy, sheeting kind of rain   washes sight

right off a window.
Fills a living room up to the ceiling,
won't pour out.

No matter how well I salt my hand, hold my breath,
and swallow.

> *The flaw on which being presses.*
> —George Oppen

—in the valley dusk   grass stills   amblers pause

silhouettes indistinct
turn trees

        lazy
              the messenger of resemblance
                        or is mind
the reluctance
while color
           fleshes every suggestion with shadow

—in the off-trail bramble

what rushes in every direction away   is time
a mouth   tonight
                hidden in ordinary   ordinal gnats

—I look too late

no rabbit in the twilit huff of dust   but
animate   is a finding-edge
                  off the fixity orbit
                        I can't entirely
displace

phenomenon opens   buries all its guests
moon
is a wall moon slips behind

—torn web   capering light   idea

still caught in its object
                  sky   of every color
                      truer than memory
coaxing eye
from plot   its refuge

—the old hunger to tell

in time's cave
            still paints animals running
on the inner lids of impatient eyes

—myths I make   sky

washing its mountain
            with evening fog   wing's voice
is wind

always the artifact   of advantage
in the vantage points   of surmise

bones to rattle
in a stone cup

THE *SPORADIC-PROVERBIAL* GRASP

> *[O]ur intellect cannot grasp Becoming, . . . and consequently
> . . . infer[s] a metaphysical world.*
> —from Friedrich Nietzsche's lectures
> on pre-Platonic philosophy

I. notes on *a theogony*

the power to systemize, coarse weave of river and clock,
desert and fingernail,
told myth and the teller's spit
cross-hatched,
the consequences of Being,
space
is a listening, twined round with words,
a strength of *I* upon *I*, call it God
as indicative of longing,
Being cannot have come to be,
the hind leg of every thought
always crouched,
a leap
to outlast the visible
—this stalking
sky

II. notes on *the power to systemize*

as if space could be carried,
cup hands and call it,
for whither would it move if it fills all space,
to swallow
is the invention of secrecy, to think a soul
all intake of breath
might be linear, the plumb line sure,
assuming our intellect is the measure of all things
to bring two
stones together
makes a god, the surfaces
perpendicular, the balance
measured, set forth
as a table, oiled with use, come
to that table, its surface waxed to mirror
a music already lost

III. notes on *assuming our intellect*

as if to steady the makeshift *we*
between us, a *sporadic-proverbial stage,*
collected like twigs,
one god
for every bundle,
one does not develop out of the other,
chew the wood through, tooth lost
in the work
becomes the word, a tension
that has no sides
might speak like a god,
in every direction, *formulations*
no longer understood by later singers
must be imagined,
just as The Sporades, two groups of Greek islands,
can't be brought into rigor, only repeatedly
applied,
nothing more helpless than a man

IV. notes on *formulations no longer understood*

in every pour is spill
tasted, the *continual blending*
of different gods,
space
isn't only a carrier, but opens like eyes,
with their hope of immortality, like supple wrists
secreting angles,
exactitude is a form of carnage,
what grazes the edge
becomes the edge, bequeaths us parameters, measures
a god margin
between everything and how to mean it

v. notes on *the continual blending of different gods*

cheese and fruit, nomadic
on a porcelain plate, *it suffices*
that we seek
a firm stroke
opens the apple, the wayward
concealed, each position will leak
other versions, *a condition*
of miserable craving, vision
blurs as it turns,
the most miraculous lawfulness of the world
catches only the heat of it
poured
as wine, the eye
must close to slice neatly into the red
sleep of action, the plate
gleams, *a justice exonerating itself of its own justice* parses
the overlapping
pressures—white square
of cheese, gold
dollop of creme, each
shapely trance

Just ink-stray and stalled thought   in the sky part
of the sentence.
Vertigo, the full rotation.   What word can face that
standing up?   No ladder
like the eye.
But where to climb? Start at one end of a sentence,
and only find the other.
Even the circle, to get somewhere,
parts from itself.   All along the border of my inescape,
the thin black line of ink
is crazed.
In the circle part of a word, of which there are many,
I adjust
the swirling surfeit mayhem of its fine machinery,
as if matter   were its observation, as if in inquiry
were attention.
In cursive,   a lackadaisical meander
following weed to cud to cattle drive
might stampede
the lethargy of necessary.
Still, no place   to part the sky of it,
to ink the infinite
into inkling.   I read the curse in cursive, recursively.
Which is a word for nervous laughter,
but doesn't like to know it.

WINDOW (CLOSED)

perspective is glass
   on a world I neither

   occupy nor contain
this red of sky

won't last the hour
   wind finds

   in trees
flock of sudden sun bracelet of red breasted blackbirds

rising
   as if something loosed in the sky stolen from landscape's

   narrow sleeve
I might clasp round my wrist

recognition
   illusory

   as it is unrelenting

FIELD NOTES: 13–16

the need to devour oneself dispenses with
the need to believe
—E. M. Cioran

—three hatchlings in the barnswallow's high-raftered nest

the absolute is a mouth
thinking
won't swallow
the fragile finality
            I make
to mean perception

—that inquisition of the always

                which I call chance
here   wobbly-headed feather tufts
their beaks answer unrelentingly
         open   measuring the illimitable
is the field
         myth I make wider
as if wider
       were a way through

—texture of lichen   dense tangents

                   touch   says the universe
as if stable
       that border color crosses
and I forget
         into expressiveness

—in the barnswallow's nest   three hatchlings

                  riffle their feathers
       phosphoresce the barn rafters away
outline mutes
what it magnifies
         into color
riding outside
      what I balance against

LOST SEQUENCE

Here's a word,
which can't stand   for other than itself,
leaning against a lamppost, drinking fortified wine.

Intoxicating elixir,   slicks down the hair
of what's definable in consciousness.

I watch.   Thirsty audience.

Bad moon
rising in the recipe.

Just the thing to which I might gleefully point.

Though direction
is cheap seduction.   The proximity of real
continually replaced.

Dust mote in the blow-by.

Writing it   makes an interesting arrest record,
but not of the actual

slurring past,
while I loiter on this side   of the already otherwise.

OF ANGLE, MORE THAN MATTER

Things appear bearing their language.
—Michel Serres

Real bodies are what never appear.
—Kathryn Bond Stockton

Square One

Desire is a mouth. No room for company inside a mouth. So much to swallow. Each morning, under the tongue a compass is spun, comes round in the end to the same direction. No means for navigating between this mouth and the mouth where I buried last night's teeth. With what, besides constancy, do we calculate? I lick your fingers to re-orient. Taste, a kind of exit, never an escape. Stealthy, what the desire for escape conceals, which lies everywhere bare before us, an erotics of the plainly spoken, yet unheard. Numb, we say, meaning we've lost ourselves at the skin-line we are endlessly factoring. Even in the mirror of zero that is touch, we count backwards, discover negative numbers. There's no end to measuring. One integer is, by definition, consumed in the next, that's all anyone gets.

Square Two

In every aspect of our relation, we hazard an equation. How to escape it? This endless counting, intimacy's avariciousness. False generosity would only complicate the means we use to estimate how much we've each already vanished. Do we call that equivalence? Scour the coffee stains on our nerves. Glue the veins in our cracked porcelain. Turn every wind-up key in our toy silences. Our church of chance and its catechisms. Do you see my eyes flash in a rain of dance or damage? Your eyes are hot afternoon in a chilled glass. I choose a lipstick to redden what we can't watch unfurl, not to outline the science we later ascribe to it. We take. Our oldest arithmetic being the shortest distance between our distances.

Back to Square One

What measure will I use tonight to fit your mouth to mine?
What means for calculating conversions is the last thought to
leave me to our bodies, our idiot savants. How soon the re-
turn. I see you're already hypothesizing data. Your fingers
against my leg. My wrist fallen across your waist. Conjecture
loves us. Always an idea in our midst, we name it flesh.
Lucretius knew, all the specifics we abstract flow right past
the transparent absolutes of a true physics. Open one eye, but
keep watch on what your other eye sees. A new angle on
clarity mirrors the old, each time differently. Beautiful cos-
tume. How well it fits. Deceived by this accident, we attempt
once again to invent order.

Four-Corner Navigation

I pull your good white shirt, now pale-pink, from the washing machine at the exact moment you do not arrive home as planned. A pink might not reflect the general condition of solids, but rather a threshold chaos through which a new physics might approach. Which is why Archimedes followed the slightest deviation along the angle of a curve and wasn't interested in simplicity. Angles are never the same angle inside the box as out. I make an angle by drawing scissors along a length of packing string before I cut it. Will I see your shirt change the color of late August's evening breeze at the same instant I decide to fold it up and hide it in a box? Good scissors must be sharp.

The Breaks

With steep angles comes brinkmanship. You offer to mea-
sure, using your hand's width, what I rant in tangents. Do I
hear only my own needs keening in each new shape I make of
appearances? Consistency is crucial, though we abjure rep-
etition. We share the science section from *The Times*. Easily
enough, print articulates in columns, but body never fits its
word. Only numbers make solution a sentence as precise as it
is endless. Impossible for us to assess our indefinite *already*
without understanding the constellation of our *as yet,* its un-
discovered planets. We spend the evening describing our
different definitions of gravity. That night,
a continuous falling
            of each belief, parallel to every other, leaves
the birdcage open in my dream, and needs
                        no bird.

MISTAKE SEQUENCE

In the miswrite of moth,   a month.
Which is the way a notebook dissembles,
and even better resembles
what most worries me.
Like your eyes   when you're listening, moth
quiet,
an only-in-profile otherness alights,
then gone,   and momentary
might be months later,
given the elliptical filler   between facts.
Comfort,
I write,   `
but didn't I mean cocoon,   what threads close
confounds the matter, meaning any next word
might be a calendar,
its compartments   squared off.
Is every practicality
stifling?
Like bars of stacked soap,
inarguable
as the interrogation   any next sentence might become,
while the notebook weighs
over and over   the same weightlessness.

CLIMATE CONDITIONAL (ONCOMING TWILIGHT)

outside in the blue cold rushing blood instructs
upward with sky

aspiring release breeds unknowing underworlds of matter
   I frighten into weather

   as if feeling were thinner and thinner of finding
what keeps

testy with talk circling some insubstance called sense
   no entrance

   only this stridence
besting its damage

dark comes
   hidden in habit

   crowd marriage of stone to storied to star to staring back
and who in the listening

dusk
   hampers what tension is needed

   to conceive difference in waking
and sleep between sound and the word

waiting for it

CAUTION SEQUENCE

Here is our new,   a window of we
between us.

Every window made

makes weather.
And this, the notebook I'd begun for stability.

Horded,   slips to *herded*,   and here is habit

fixing the teeth of each new fear   on the tail of the last,
as if safe

in that cursive
of endless talk.   Where you begin, I must have left off.
Covetous

of the malfeasance, never a missed
affliction   in affection.

No is an outside word, moves the highway closer to the house.
I tumble
three windows into one,
but still can't fit head and shoulders through,

knowing that the narrow   is needle's eye, cliché-ish,
conjectural.
Sewing thread can be used

only as trope.

Wasn't the startle of your actual eye   what I'd come here
to inhabit?

To trust the quickness

with which everything I've fixed around us vanishes.

POSITIONS OF THE DANCE

every form is draped in an affinity of adherences
—Michel Serres

Rehearsal

—I watch you,   new

                                        gravity, enacted
                                        as inevitable.
Enticing,
with the witchery of flesh,

                                        destruction.

To the guile of perspective

                                        the eye cleaves.
A dancer can't

encompass the grief   achieved in horizon.
                                        Must enter his own eye
                                                flying.

Outside the studio window, just before impact,
                                three barnswallows turn
the color of chance
wind
                        chills the skin. Your arms would outreach

the body's imbricate fears, feather upon feather,

the wing   we know as flesh.

The dead
walk their mountain.

The body wanders,
the length of its reach

                                excrement and air
                                  two finite harbors

we travel between
your hands

                        the bedrock and brittle of bone—

Balance

                                        —on the studio worktable
rosin chips, sweat bands, drying leaves, two angular stones
tied together with string,
                                                    leaning
                                        larger the absence

between them. Their object is not stillness,
their stillness
is not refusal. Missive of stones
                                        sent from silence
                                through your arched body,
                            your outstretched, open palms.

Your eyes wear me
watching you,
until what I am   is worn through.
                                                    Brief,
                            any outpouring of infinite
must bend
                with the eye's concealments,

must belie the surgeries of gesture
                                lost in a line.
Even the widest arc
is remnant   of mistaking thought
                            for thread, face for fable.

                                                    Don't we think
                                        to fix
                                                    with intention,
to make of an act   idea.

Its burial site

is language,   hand with hand,   lip with lip, stone
                                                                      with stone.

We lie down on the studio floor
                                        and drift,

bodies on the world's back—

Unremitting, the Dance

—the veins of an act must be
intractable, but directive
                                        as sudden rain
is a weight more fluid
than any attempt to contain it—a torso shifts, arms draw in, an
ankle turns

the dance,   a woman
is quietly leading her children through a door, or a night, or
a fierce shapelessness

into aftermath—
breath hides behind her cupped hands,

is she cautioning her children to stay close

                                        under a small blanket of minutes
she has knit
to cover them—here,
aren't you
                                                  flowing back
down rivulets in a storm,

carrying your own bread, clothes, mortality in a small
rainsoaked bundle—the veins
of an act will remain.   Remain flowing

with the burning   and acceleration of stars
lit with kerosene, with
gods, with men following

a woman
who has already become transparent
as words,

                         our shadowboxes of wind, with walls
                              of the thinnest future—

Threnody

—masked in movement, how little the body admits. Veiled
but for a stitch
                        catching the rib
quickening
touch. The hidden wrists
in chance.
Lifted ankle, lowered chin,
mistaken glance,
mortality

grows daily
in our nails and hair.
The daily is a window   impenetrable as daylight.
                                        Strike it,
what rings against our flesh, pure
                                tonal embrace.
A sound our ears hear

into transparence.
Sink the stone of any answer
                        under your tongue—

As If Already Elsewhere

                                        —your uplifting arms
disrupt,   usurp,

                                        grasp the invisible

bird
landing   inside the visible.

                                        Throw a motion
in dance, and it falls
                                        as a blanket might careen

from windy hillside

                                        might, as *careen*,
caress the out-swaying beyond

                                        as sky's curtain of movement
is light
upward in a wind

of knuckle and hip and knee
                        turning   collapse into
a calendar

                                        and where the days
tear loose, rise, the undulant

bird of it
leaps outside wing, that haphazard

                    is splendor's resolute

malfunction, terror is a sky of it

the observer must see through
what the eye is,

              finding her way again and again

outside of the one thing—

Climate Conditional (late watch)

    try the window night
with saying

so obvious
    the boundary merely aggrieved

    little threats of theatre I throw down after the dream
is already cold

surface
    is its memorized plan

    smooth
I said not meaning smothered

but lose my nerve
    choose cunning

    trusty scout
endlessly enroute

as if travel between true and the town of true
    were enough

    effort swallowed up sunrise with surmise
of expanse at the expense of sight

I nearly miss the pale lavender almost blue cosmos
    full headed flowering

tall wind leaning in the narrow patch of the neighbor's yard
murmuring

at the same register and speed
 of my own

 indecipherable exchange

MORNING SEQUENCE

Heater's noise, while saying the same thing, doesn't
repeat itself.
This in the early chill, still under the covers

of bedroom's changing faces, each expression   ambiguous.

Nothing like the frown a kitchen wears,   clean plates,
dirty plates, the same.
Industrious frown,
like the good, swift clap of two hands together, just once.

The ready,
always louder than the thing done.

Place self here, but where exactly,   qualifiers coquettish.
Bemused.

Sentences busily bracketing,
but really there's no getting any farther inside the house
or out.

In the notebook for bedroom, maybe by afternoon,
empty spaciousness   almost legible,

when evidence was what I'd counted on,
counted up,
contrived into better objects than the objects
themselves.   As with saying

the sheets are clean, the vacuuming done.

So as to avoid the quiet implacable,
its ironic disdain. A *familiarity*   that might almost
be mistaken for *friendly*.
Mask

loves to spy a mask, but   *recognize* isn't
reckoned with.

Unsteadily, into confusion is best   left expressionless.

> *Perhaps the most important word is "and."*
> —Rosmarie Waldrop

—first sunrise with no fog

morning thoughts
                gang-up assault on visibility
mind's furtive math
collects every hiss and crackle
walking the gravel path
                    gravity repeatedly mistaken
                          for ground
as dawn's working
notion for what happens
                incorporates all options

—a stone tossed high

is replaced by the one that's caught
my eye
                catches only brief startle
reflex of sky
                    rebalancing
the everything into which I'm already
replaced
                    not even one cloud
but here is sky after sky

—lichen on stone   arguing matter for paradise

each silhouette elegant   deathless
                                along a surface scar
the circuit swells its soundlessness
I insert concealment
                        no surfeit
                        like the linear

—lichen   the fungal body

dense bewilderments   call it purpose

                to anchor and   as if from   nothing

absorb

NOTES

Between 1872 and 1876 Friedrich Nietzsche delivered a series of lectures on the progression of philosophic insight from Thales to Socrates. All italicized phrases in "The *sporadic-proverbial* Grasp" are derived from a translation of these lectures by Greg Whitlock, published with commentary under the title *The Pre-Platonic Philosophers* (University of Illinois Press, 2000).

"Positions of the Dance" is a response to collaborations between visual artist Rosario Lopez (Bogotá, Colombia) & dancer/choreographer Christopher Williams (New York City), which occurred while we were on fellowships at the Djerassi Resident Artists Program in August 2002. These collaborations became the mixed media work *Piedras,* which premiered in March 2004 at La Casa del Teatro Nacional in Bogotá, Colombia. *Piedras,* originally conceived by Lopez, included Lopez's video presentations; Williams's choreography, performed by Williams and Andrei Garzon; and my poems, sung by soprano Juanita Delgado.